THE VOICE OF FOOTBALL

CW01651466

FOOTBALL LEGENDS

CHLOE KELLY

WRITTEN BY KEVIN PETTMAN
ILLUSTRATED BY JAMIE ORRELL

PUFFIN

PUFFIN BOOKS
UK | USA | Canada | Ireland | Australia
India | New Zealand | South Africa
Puffin Books is part of the Penguin Random House group of companies
whose addresses can be found at global.penguinrandomhouse.com
www.penguin.co.uk www.puffin.co.uk www.ladybird.co.uk

Penguin Random House UK

First published 2026
001
Written by Kevin Pettman

Illustrations of footballers and full-scene artworks by Jamie Orrell

Printed in Great Britain by Clays Ltd, Elcograf S.p.A.
The authorized representative in the EEA is Penguin Random House Ireland,
Morrison Chambers, 32 Nassau Street, Dublin D02 YH68

A CIP catalogue record for this book is available from the British Library
ISBN: 978-0-241-81218-1

All correspondence to:
Puffin Books, Penguin Random House Children's
One Embassy Gardens, 8 Viaduct Gardens, London SW11 7BW

FSC www.fsc.org MIX Paper FSC® C018179

Penguin Random House is committed to a sustainable future for our business, our readers and our planet. This book is made from Forest Stewardship Council® certified paper.

Acknowledgements
The quotations on p.4, p.7, p.13, p.16, p.18, p.19, p.22, p.26, p.31, p.37, p.41, p.47, p.65 and p.71 are taken from interviews, press conferences and publicly available articles and video recordings. The author and publisher are grateful to the journalists, broadcasters and organisations who produced these materials.

Full publication details are available at:
https://www.penguin.co.uk/discover/childrens-articles/shoot-football-legends-chloe-kelly-references

CONTENTS

INTRODUCTION

Chloe Kelly is a total FOOTBALL LEGEND!

With stunning goals, awesome assists, cool penalties and game-changing skills, she's a superstar for club and country.

Chloe's power in the penalty box won Euro 2025 and Euro 2022 for England's women. She also came close to World Cup success in 2023. The electric forward is a Champions League winner and Women's Super League (WSL) icon.

This book reveals everything you need to know about the legendary Lioness and is brought to you by ***SHOOT*** – the voice of football.

Turn the page to KICK OFF your **Chloe Kelly** adventure!

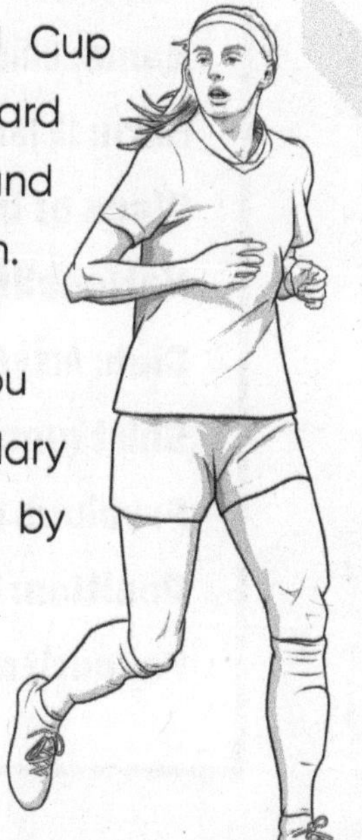

CHLOE KELLY

FACT FILE

Name: Chloe Maggie Kelly

Born: 15 January 1998

Place of birth: London, United Kingdom

Nationality: English

Club: Arsenal

Shirt number: 18

Previous clubs: Manchester City and Everton

Position: Left wing/right wing

Favourite foot: Right

STATS*

WSL games: 143

WSL goals: 43

WSL assists: 37

England games: 65

England goals: 9

International trophies: 4

RATINGS

Attack: 90/100

Dribbling: 91/100

Speed: 89/100

Passing: 86/100

Defence: 44/100

Overall: 87/100

LEGEND RATING:

★★★★★★★★★☆

9/10 STARS

* Correct at time of publication

CHAPTER 1

KELLY THE KID

Chloe Kelly grew up in Ealing, west London, UK. She started playing football at the age of four, often against her FIVE OLDER BROTHERS.

Her mum said she "always had a ball at her feet"!

+++++++++

Near **Chloe's** home was a small tarmac pitch with metal fences called the CAGE. Sounds scary, but talented and tough **Chloe** played there all the time.

She was the only girl, and her displays in the cage were EPIC.

+++++++++

Chloe's favourite team was Queens Park Rangers (QPR). Watching their games at Loftus Road Stadium was such a blast for the footy-mad youngster.

Her favourite player in the world? Not **Messi** or **Ronaldo**, but the brilliant QPR attacker **Adel Taarabt**! **Chloe** loved his silky skills and entertaining style.

She watched YouTube clips of the Moroccan's magical tricks to learn how to copy his moves. The Ealing kid wanted to do the same eye-catching moves one day on the biggest stage.

Aged eight, the energetic and street-smart girl was thrilled to join the QPR youth team. In their blue-and-white kit, she quickly developed her game and learned loads from the coaches.

Her Under-10 team was undefeated for TWO YEARS! **Chloe** won team trophies and individual prizes.

A QPR coach said, "She always had a beaming smile . . . She was playing for the club that she dearly loves."

++++++++++

Another of **Chloe's** heroes at the time was England and Arsenal striker **Kelly Smith**.

As well as scoring 46 GOALS for her country, **Smith** was a strong leader and lethal finisher.

Chloe read **Smith's** book and watched her play as much as possible to pick up scoring tips.

Chloe didn't know it back then, but one day in the future she would get to play in the SAME TEAM as **Smith**. Better yet, the two would become friends as well!

+++++++++

Chloe enjoyed working with the QPR coaches. She practised and played every week with her young teammates. To sharpen her ball control, she did KEEPIE-UPPIES.

+++++++++

It's fun to count how many keepie-uppies you can do before the ball touches the ground!

Ready for a **Chloe Kelly** keepie-uppie challenge . . . ?

CHLOE KELLY KEEPIE-UPPIE CHALLENGE

1. Find a ball. It can be a full-size football or a small soft one, or maybe a tennis ball if you fancy more of a challenge!

2. With an adult, find a safe outdoor space with plenty of room all around you.

3. Begin doing keepie-uppies. Use either foot, or either of your knees, to keep the ball up in the air without touching the ground. Take it slowly, and build your confidence.

4. Keep practising! Do this for two minutes a day, for five days.

5. Scribble your keepie-uppie record for each day on the chart on the next page.

☐ **DAY 1**

I did _____ keepie-uppies.

☐ **DAY 2**

I did _____ keepie-uppies.

☐ **DAY 3**

I did _____ keepie-uppies.

☐ **DAY 4**

I did _____ keepie-uppies.

☐ **DAY 5**

I did _____ keepie-uppies.

What's your best daily score?

0–4	Great start, keep going!
5–10	Not bad, baller!
11–20	Incredible silky skills!
21 or more	That's total **Chloe Kelly** quality!

+++++++++

Even though she was a huge QPR fan, after four years **Chloe** decided to leave the club. Her TOP TALENT meant she needed to play with and against other top girls.

+++++++++

Arsenal are one of the world's best clubs. Joining the Gunners' academy was perfect, and **Chloe** made the switch aged 12.

It was a big commitment. Training with Arsenal meant **Chloe** had to take a TWO-HOUR TRAIN JOURNEY across London after school. It was 11 pm by the time she got home again – and then there was school the next day.

Chloe did it because she wanted to be the BEST.

Luckily, on the train ride she had a friend – future club and country teammate **Lotte Wubben-Moy**! The pair spent a lot of time together as teenagers with Arsenal.

All **Chloe's** hard work was rewarded. While playing in youth teams alongside **Leah Williamson** – another future legend – **Chloe** impressed the coaches and got to train with the senior squad.

That meant being on the same pitch as . . .

. . . **Chloe's** hero, **Kelly Smith**!

Smith was still playing for the Gunners then, and **Chloe** was a bit scared to get close to her childhood idol.

But, thanks to her talent, **Chloe** soon looked right at home alongside Arsenal's experienced professionals. She learned from other older stars, including **Rachel Yankey**, **Casey Stoney** and **Fara Williams**.

"**Chloe** was a young kid full of energy, wanting to prove how good she potentially could be," said **Kelly Smith**, describing the first time she saw **Chloe** play.

It was a rapid rise through the Arsenal ranks for **Chloe**, and she was also excelling with the England youth teams.

+++++++++

Usually, **Chloe** played as a central striker – it wasn't until later that she became a dazzling wide forward. Her match intelligence was already sharp, and she had superb vision and movement.

+++++++++

By the time she celebrated her 17th birthday, **Chloe** felt ready to burst on to the scene and make her mark for Arsenal.

CHAPTER 2

PROFESSIONAL PLAYER

TWENTY-TWO MINUTES. That's all it took for **Chloe** to score in her first senior game for Arsenal!

Her exciting debut goal came in a League Cup match against Watford in July 2015. At the age of just 17, **Chloe** showed exactly why she would become one of the world's best attackers.

The finish was a precise header from

close range, pouncing on a cross into the box from teammate **Danielle Carter**, making it 2–0.

The Gunners eventually won 3–0.

Chloe was happy. After the match she said, "It was great. I was a bit nervous at the start, going into the game. I grew in confidence with the players behind me."

Other players in the Arsenal line-up included **Leah Williamson**, who also scored, and defender **Lotte Wubben-Moy**, who was making her debut too!

Just after her 18th birthday, **Chloe** signed her first professional contract with Arsenal. The teenager was dreaming of more games and goals.

+++++++++

In May 2016, Arsenal reached the Women's FA Cup final, facing London rivals Chelsea at Wembley.

Arsenal won 1–0, but **Chloe** didn't get on the pitch and wasn't even on the substitutes' bench.

She was super keen to play matches. So, in June 2016, she went to Everton on loan. There, she netted TWO goals in NINE appearances, as Everton pushed for promotion to the top league.

When she returned to Arsenal, **Chloe** again struggled for league games. She agreed to another loan to Everton for the 2017/18 season and soon . . .

BANGED IN THE GOALS!

A HAT-TRICK – the first of her senior career – came against Oxford United. That made it SEVEN goals in her first 11 games that season.

Time for a BIG DECISION. Things were going well at Everton, so **Chloe** joined permanently in January 2018.

A sad goodbye to Arsenal . . . but maybe she'd return one day?

+++++++++

When she transferred to Everton, **Chloe** said, "The first time I came to this club, I really loved it. I knew it was somewhere I wanted to call home, and I'm really happy."

The Everton supporters really liked what **Chloe** could do on the pitch. She gave defenders big problems with her pace and clever movement.

The forward was only 20 years old, but she had excellent composure and quick thinking in front of goal.

At the same time as **Chloe** left Arsenal for Merseyside, so did one of her friends and England Under-20 teammates – attacking full back or wing back **Taylor Hinds**!

They had enjoyed playing together in the youth teams for both Arsenal and the Lionesses.

Chloe felt it was a great move for **Taylor** to come to the young team at Everton. "I'm looking forward to being on the pitch with her again," she said.

GOOD VIBES ALL ROUND!

+++++++++

An ankle injury ended **Chloe's** 2018/19 season early, but after recovering she was back with a bang for Everton in 2019/20.

In just her second WSL match, **Chloe** slammed in TWO QUALITY GOALS against Bristol City.

A rifled right-foot shot, after cutting in from the left and beating defenders.

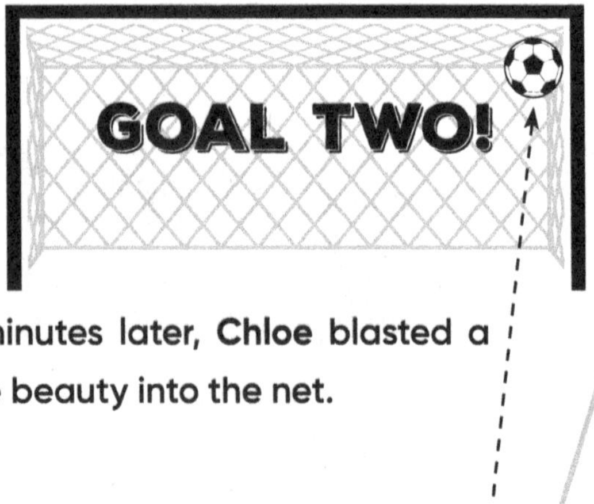

Just two minutes later, Chloe blasted a long-range beauty into the net.

Chloe's devastating double went viral on social media!

+++++++++

A deep breath, a high knee, a leap and then a fast run-up before striking the ball.

That's **Chloe's** PENALTY TECHNIQUE, and it's one of the TOP THINGS about her game. She first began using this unusual method of scoring from the spot while playing for Everton.

"I can't explain it too much. It's just my routine that works for me," **Chloe** has said about the way she takes a pen.

Here's your chance to be a penalty legend, too, with the special . . .

. . . KELLY KICK.

1. With an adult, find a local park or playground with a football pitch. If there isn't a pitch, then make your own using jumpers or bags as goalposts.

2. Put the ball on the penalty spot, but spin it back a few times as you place it.

3. Stand still and raise your knee. (Chloe lifts her left knee, but you do you!)

4. Bring your knee down, then take quick strides as you run forward.

5. Strike the ball with the inside of your foot to powerfully place the ball to the right or left.

+++++++++

Later in the 2019/20 season, there came another memorable match for Everton's star scorer. Against Reading in the WSL, **Chloe** bagged another brilliant HAT-TRICK.

Scoring straight from a corner is very rare . . . but that's exactly what **Chloe** did! She whipped in a bending corner, and it flew directly into the net beyond the stunned Reading goalkeeper.

That was the second of **Chloe's** THREE GOALS that day. She was fast becoming a WSL HERO.

CHAPTER 3

ENGLAND ADVENTURE

Playing for England was always a dream for **Chloe**.

As a youngster, she sometimes took a bus to Wembley when a big match was on. **Chloe** didn't have a match ticket, but she just loved the stadium's vibe.

Could she really play there herself one day and become an England STAR?

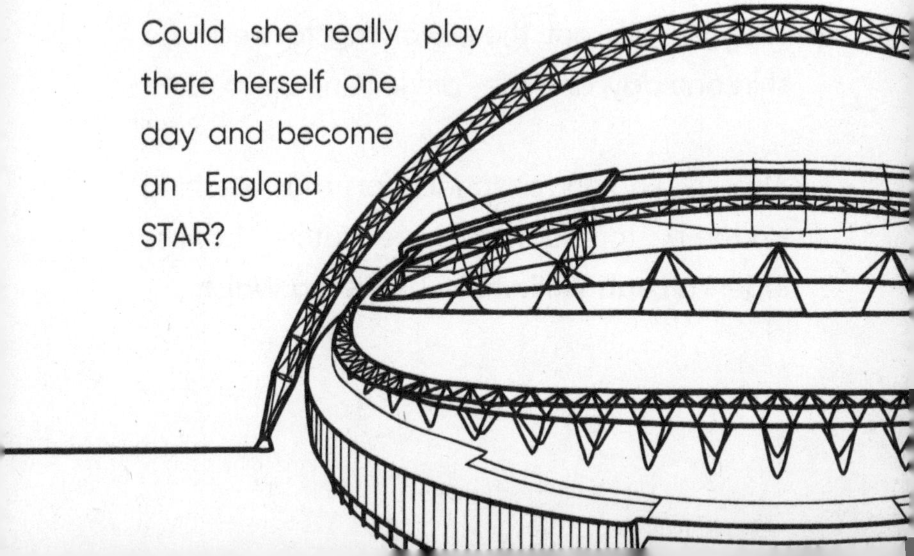

Thanks to **Chloe's** talent and desire to be the very best, she got an early chance to shine for the Lionesses.

She was picked for the England Under-15 team in 2011, and quickly moved up through the age levels.

In 2013, **Chloe** was part of the team that reached the semi-final of the UEFA Under-17 championship.

As England progressed in that event, **Chloe** said, "It's important to keep raising awareness of women's football. We know there are younger girls out there wanting to wear the shirt one day, and they are looking up to us."

Also in England's squad for that exciting Under-17 tournament were future Lioness legends **Leah Williamson** and **Keira Walsh**.

Alongside her teammates, **Chloe** was becoming an even better player. As well as **Lotte Wubben-Moy**, **Chloe's** England youth teammates over the years also included **Alessia Russo** and **Georgia Stanway**.

The players grew up as good friends, and shared a strong bond when they all wore the England shirt together.

Chloe was becoming a LEADER for her country.

At the UEFA Under-17 competition in 2015, she was made the TEAM CAPTAIN for ENGLAND. Wearing the captain's armband for her country was a very proud moment for the young player!

+++++++++

In 2018, her international journey with England went up another level. Stepping on to the pitch at a World Cup is huge – and **Chloe** was about to experience just that at the FIFA Under-20 World Cup in France.

The Under-20 World Cup was the biggest test yet for **Chloe** . . . and she SMASHED it, as usual!

She played in ALL THREE of England's group games, and they remained undefeated against North Korea, Brazil and Mexico. A goal in the HUGE 6–1 win over Mexico was a great reward for her.

In the quarter-final, **Chloe** and the other young Lionesses defeated the Netherlands to reach the semi-final for the first time.

With fans cheering them on in northwest France, England lost 2–0 to a strong Japan team, who then went on to win the final. **Chloe** could still celebrate, though, after beating France to finish in third place! She played in every game, and looked seriously SLICK taking on some of the best young defenders in the world.

And her FIFA Under-20 World Cup adventure was the best preparation for what was about to happen . . .

++++++++++

Three months later, **Chloe** got a SURPRISE CALL-UP to the ENGLAND FIRST TEAM! The plan was for her to train with the squad, just to get some experience with the senior players . . .

But then **Chloe** discovered she would be on the substitutes' bench for their friendly match away to Austria!

Still in shock, the 20-year-old joined the match for the final 11 minutes.

The occasion was a LOT to take in.

"My legs were like jelly!" she later said, admitting to having been very nervous.

Chloe even had a chance in front of goal, but Austria's goalkeeper and a defender made good blocks to stop her scoring.

Georgia Stanway and **Chioma Ubogagu** also made their debuts, both scoring in the 3–0 win.

+++++++++

Chloe's next target? Playing at the 2019 World Cup, but she sadly WASN'T PICKED to play at that competition!

Chloe knew that she needed to keep working hard and

playing well to become a regular in the England team.

+++++++++

After another top season, with NINE goals in 12 WSL games for Everton in 2019/20, **Chloe** decided to leave in June 2020.

Manchester City was her next club. Her QUEST TO BE THE BEST continued!

NAME GAME

Fill in the missing letters on the page opposite to spell the names of players also in the squad when Chloe made her England debut in 2018.

Now, put the missing letters together to spell another player's surname:

_ _ _ _ _

Answers on page 74.

CHAPTER 4

MANCHESTER MOVE

Arriving at Manchester City in summer 2020 was another step up for the rising star.

Chloe was given SHIRT NUMBER 9 – an iconic number for a goalscorer to have the honour of wearing.

City had a squad packed with talent. Already at the club were **Ellen White**, **Steph Houghton**, **Georgia Stanway**, **Lauren Hemp**, **Keira Walsh** and

Esme Morgan. And, shortly after **Chloe** joined, her England teammates **Lucy Bronze** and **Alex Greenwood** also did.

++++++++++

Chloe's first two WSL goals for City came in a 4–1 win over Tottenham.

She cracked in a LONG-RANGE shot after bringing the ball inside from the left. **Chloe** then buried a powerful penalty in the second half, using her reliable spot-kick technique.

Playing as a winger, **Chloe** was free to speed through the middle and link with the central striker. It was a fantastic start in Manchester!

++++++++++

Due to the COVID-19 pandemic, the 2020 FA Cup final was played early in the 2020/21 season . . . against Everton!

How would **Chloe** get on playing against the team she had left just A FEW MONTHS earlier?

The match was staged at Wembley – **Chloe's** favourite stadium – and it was very close.

Playing in a front three alongside England striker **Ellen White** and USA World Cup winner **Rose Lavelle**, **Chloe** looked very sharp.

City were ahead . . .

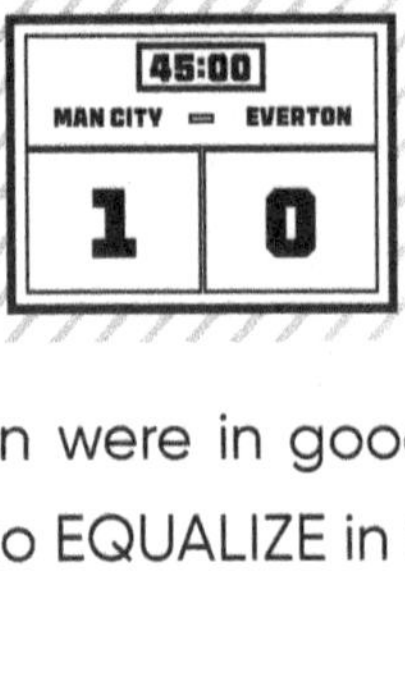

AT HALF-TIME!

Everton were in good shape though, battling back to EQUALIZE in the 60th minute.

City had chances to win in the 90 minutes, but EXTRA TIME was needed. With a penalty shoot-out looking likely, it was City substitutes

Georgia Stanway and **Janine Beckie** who grabbed BIG GOALS with just minutes left.

City celebrated a 3–1 FA Cup final victory.

Chloe already had her FIRST TROPHY with the club!

"It's something dreams are made of," she said.

+++++++++

The Champions League is a tournament every player wants to be in. Facing EUROPE'S TOP TEAMS in dramatic matches is so exciting.

At Manchester City, **Chloe** finally had her chance to take part. It was another reason why she wanted to be a City player.

Her Champions League debut match was against Swedish club BK Häcken in the round of 32.

City won both legs against Häcken, then beat Italians Fiorentina with an aggregate score of 8–0 across both games.

Next up in **Chloe's** European journey was a quarter-final against Barcelona!

The forward had been full of goals and assists all season, but playing the SPANISH GIANTS was tough.

Unfortunately Manchester City lost the away first leg 3–0 and, to make matters worse, **Chloe** MISSED a penalty in the match.

A 2–1 win for City in the second leg wasn't enough to put the club into the semi-finals.

It was a RARE LOW in **Chloe's** brilliant City season.

+++++++++

Chloe's mission now was to fire City to the WSL title ahead of Chelsea.

She scored in the 2–2 draw with the Londoners. With only two games left, City were two points behind Chelsea.

Then, just when her team needed her most, **Chloe** suffered a terrible INJURY!

It came in a 4–0 win over Birmingham.

She had scored twice, but fell in pain as she ran to try for her third goal . . .

. . . BAD NEWS!

A serious injury to **Chloe's** right knee affecting her anterior cruciate ligament (ACL) ended her season. She would be out for a LONG TIME. It was a devastating blow.

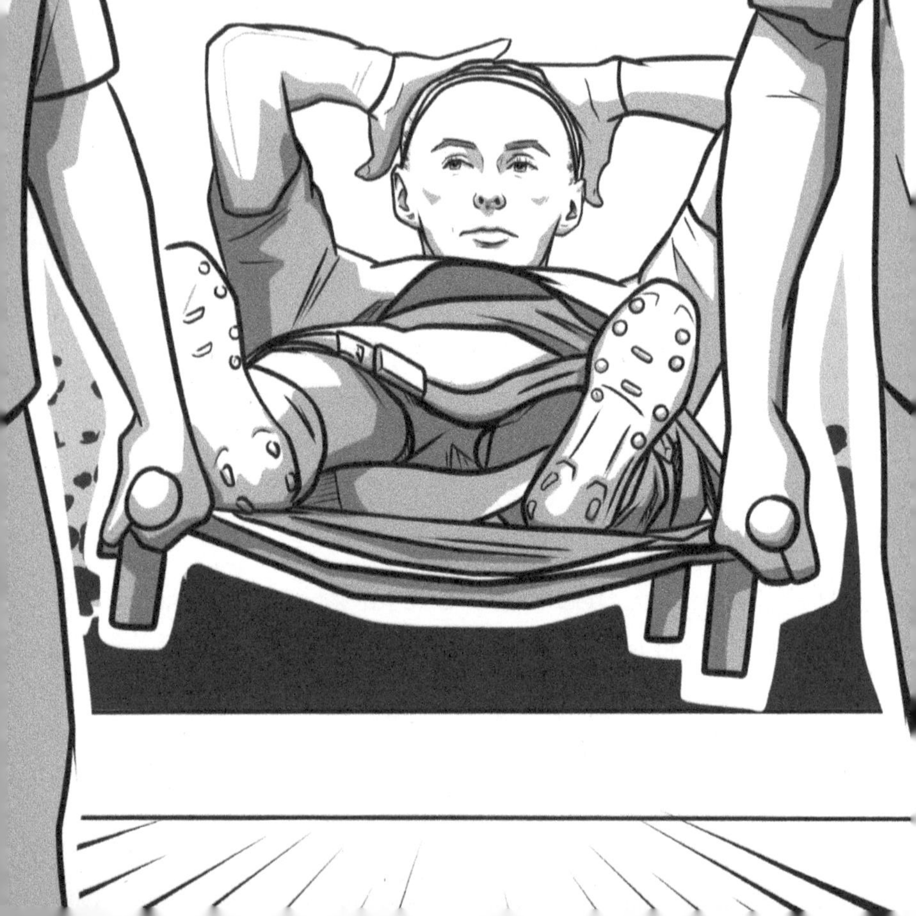

With **Chloe** injured, City had one WSL game left to play.

City won, beating West Ham 1–0, but Chelsea finished as champions. City were RUNNERS-UP.

Chloe's first season at the club saw 16 GOALS and 14 ASSISTS in 34 GAMES.

Her next big battle? To get fit and back on the pitch.

As well as missing lots of games for Manchester City in the 2021/22 season, **Chloe** was also out of the international matches. She had looked certain to play for Great Britain at the Olympics in 2021, but her cruel injury ruined that hope.

"There were so many times when I just sat and cried," she later said about it. "All I know is playing football."

TRUE OR FALSE?

How much can you remember about Chloe's first City season? Tick the correct box beside each statement.

	TRUE	FALSE
1. Chloe wore shirt number 9.		
2. She beat Arsenal in the FA Cup final.		
3. Her Champions League debut was against Barcelona.		
4. Chloe scored 16 goals in total during the season.		
5. She got injured playing Aston Villa.		

Answers on page 74.

CHAPTER 5

AWESOME EUROS

The knee injury was tough for **Chloe**. It took her 11 MONTHS to get back to full fitness.

She watched on as her Manchester City teammates beat Chelsea to win the 2021/22 League Cup final.

AT LAST, in April 2022, **Chloe** played her first game since the injury. She came on as a substitute in City's 2–0 WSL win at West Ham.

What a fantastic feeling being . . .

BACK ON THE PITCH!

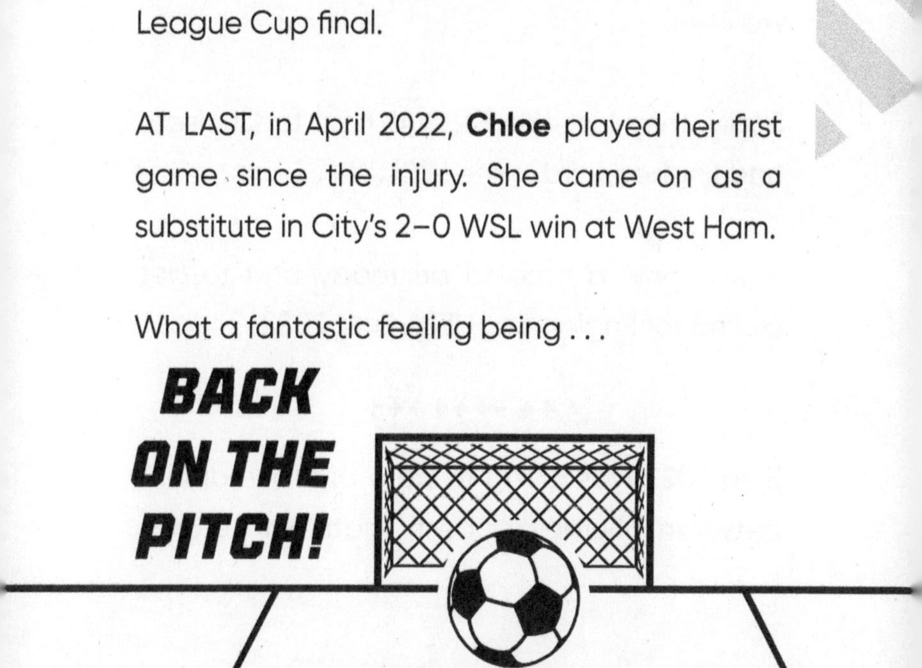

Just two weeks later, **Chloe** scored her FIRST GOAL of the season.

It was another clash with West Ham, this time in the FA Cup semi-final. She pounced on a mistake in the defence to coolly slot the ball past the goalkeeper.

Chloe enjoyed the celebrations, and City won 4–1.

Sadly, they lost the FA Cup final to Chelsea, and finished third in the WSL.

It was now a race to be ready and to get picked for England at UEFA Euro 2022.

+++++++++

Euro 2022 was going to be a big tournament between Europe's best national teams.

Chloe was desperate to play, especially as the competition was in England.

But first, she had to show the new England manager, **Sarina Wiegman**, that she was back to her best in attack.

+++++++++

Chloe got her chance in a friendly game with Belgium in June. She came on in the second half, and scored her first senior . . .

ENGLAND GOAL!

AND THAT'S A
FINE FINISH FROM
CHLOE KELLY!
18

"I said from the minute I got injured that I wanted to be at the Euros," **Chloe** later explained.

Wiegman was very happy to see **Chloe** scoring and making an impact. The manager picked her to be in the 23-player Euros squad!

It was BRILLIANT NEWS, and **Chloe** was buzzing.

England's first game of the competition was against Austria on 6 July. The dream was to go all the way, and to win the final on 31 July.

+++++++++

England won FIVE GAMES in a row to reach the Euro 2022 final!

WIN ONE

Beth Mead scored, and Chloe came on as a second-half sub.

WIN TWO

FT	
ENGLAND	NORWAY
8	0

A goal-fest with five different scorers! Chloe joined the match in the 70th minute.

WIN THREE

The Lionesses topped their group, and Chloe replaced Lauren Hemp in the 60th minute.

FT	
ENGLAND	N. IRELAND
5	0

WIN FOUR

FT	
ENGLAND	SPAIN
2	1

A dramatic extra-time quarter-final win in which Chloe again played as a substitute.

WIN FIVE

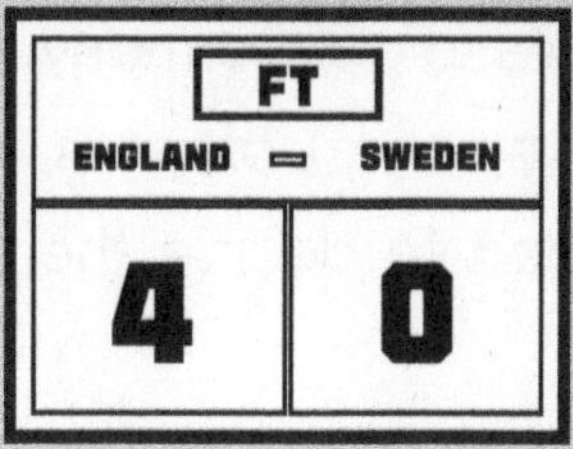

The Lionesses were 4–0 up when **Chloe** played for the last four minutes in the semi-final.

ENGLAND HAD REACHED THE FINAL.

Chloe played every game as a sub, and hadn't scored yet. But her winning Wembley moment was on its way . . .

++++++++++

England faced Germany in the EURO 2022 FINAL in front of 87,000 fans and MILLIONS watching on television.

Ella Toone put England 1–0 ahead in the second half. As soon as the goal was scored,

Sarina Wiegman brought **Chloe** on as a substitute. With just 11 minutes to go, Germany equalized! This really knocked the Lionesses, and EXTRA TIME was needed to decide the winner.

Chloe came to the rescue . . .

. . . when she POKED THE BALL INTO THE NET from close range in the 110th minute!

It was a SCRAPPY GOAL from a corner, but that didn't matter one bit – the crowd and England's players went wild! **Chloe** ripped off her shirt and swung it over her head as she screamed and jumped around with her teammates.

The final whistle blew shortly after.

Chloe's MAGIC TOUCH had won the match.

THE LIONESSES WERE EURO 2022 CHAMPIONS!

The whole country celebrated England's UNBELIEVABLE victory.

Chloe's WINNING GOAL captured a major trophy for England for the FIRST TIME since the men had won the 1966 World Cup. She was the HERO, and it was extra special to score the goal at Wembley – the stadium she'd worshipped since she was a kid!

The shirt-waving celebration will never be forgotten, either. It was an ICONIC MOMENT from an iconic player. **Chloe** had delivered on the biggest stage. And this was just the beginning!

GAME CHANGER

There are FIVE DIFFERENCES between these two pictures of Chloe celebrating her Euro 2022 winner.

Can you spot them all?

Answers on page 74.

CHAPTER 6

WORLD STAR

Chloe Kelly was now one of the BEST SCORERS on the planet.

She had everything – big game skills, awesome match-winning penalties and a desire to keep getting better.

After her Euro 2022 heroics, the next mission was for England to win the brand-new Finalissima trophy. This was a special one-game final in April 2023 between the champions of Europe and the champions of South America – Brazil.

ANOTHER COLOSSAL CLASH AT WEMBLEY!

Beating the brilliant Brazilians would not be easy, even with over 80,000 fans cheering England on.

Chloe started on the substitutes' bench once again. Then, in the 74th minute, she replaced **Lauren James** in attack.

The Lionesses were 1–0 up after **Ella Toone** scored in the first half. With only seconds left to play, the Finalissima was set to be another big prize for England . . .

Until Brazil scored, and the match went to PENALTIES!

Could England's players and supporters handle another HUGE Wembley penalty shoot-out?

The first eight penalties were NAIL-BITING!

Georgia Stanway	Ella Toone	Rachel Daly	Alex Greenwood
SCORED	SAVED	SCORED	SCORED

Adriana	Tamires	Rafaelle Souza	Kerolin
SCORED	SAVED	MISSED	SCORED

England were 3–2 up when **Chloe** calmly walked forward to take England's fifth penalty. IF SHE SCORED, ENGLAND WOULD WIN.

Chloe placed the ball down, stamped each foot either side of it, and took six steps back. She took a deep breath, raised her left knee, and jumped forward into her run-up . . .

...SMASH!

The ball was struck hard to the left, beyond the fingertips of Brazil's goalkeeper and into the net.

Chloe had won the Finalissima! Her teammates dashed to celebrate with her. Another MASSIVE moment for the Lionesses.

+++++++++

Playing at a World Cup is the ULTIMATE GOAL for every footballer.

Chloe had starred at the Under-20 World Cup back in 2018.

In 2023, just a few months after winning the Finalissima, she was ready to help England go all the way at her first senior World Cup – Australia and New Zealand 2023.

Would **Chloe's** 20 goal involvements – 14 ASSISTS and SIX GOALS – for Manchester City be good enough for her to start for England?

YES THEY WOULD!

Chloe started the first two group games as the Lionesses BEAT Haiti and Denmark.

She came off the bench to score in the final group game, a 6–1 SMASHING of China.

Next, England BATTLED Nigeria in the round of 16 knockout game. **Chloe** was called up from the bench in the second half, and the close game finished 0–0.

Penalties would decide who reached the World Cup quarter-finals . . .

Can you guess who scored the winning shoot-out spot kick against Nigeria? **Chloe Kelly** again, of course!

Her SUPER STRIKE following her famous penalty run-up routine put England into the quarter-finals with Colombia.

She helped the Lionesses beat the mighty South Americans 2–1 to set up a SEMI-FINAL with host-team Australia.

Chloe only played the last few minutes against Australia, but ENGLAND WON 3–1 . . .

. . . and reached the World Cup final for the FIRST TIME!

An extremely talented Spain were their opponents in the final.

Sadly, England struggled to get the better of Spain, and were 1–0 BEHIND by half-time.

Chloe came off the bench at the start of the second half, but this time she couldn't work her magic.

Losing the final was so difficult to take. Lifting that trophy would've been the best feeling.

+++++++++

It had been a breath-taking year for **Chloe** and her England teammates.

Losing the 2023 World Cup final was gut-wrenching, but England were still proud to be runners-up. Plus, there were the Euro 2022 and Finalissima successes to celebrate!

+++++++++

Back at Manchester City, **Chloe** hit eight goals and seven assists in 2023/24, including a WONDER GOAL against Liverpool in the League Cup.

But the season after that at Manchester City would be very different.

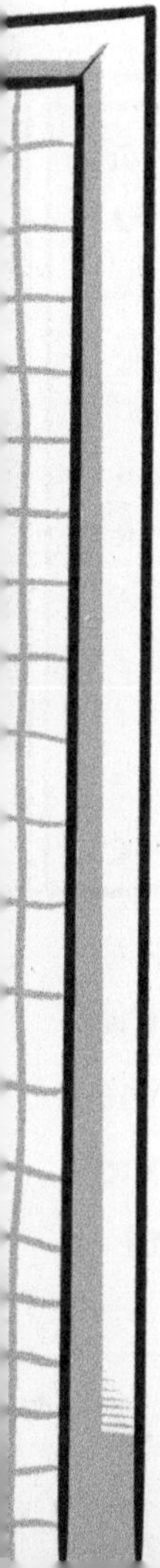

TEAM TRACKER

Hidden in the goal net are the seven teams Chloe played against at the 2023 World Cup. Can you find them all? Answers can go across or down.

S	W	E	W	E	Y	Q	P	C	Y	C	E	U	G	Q	Z	J	Q
V	D	Y	F	L	C	O	L	O	M	B	I	A	J	T	H	A	U
F	B	Y	U	N	I	G	E	R	I	A	G	W	I	B	C	N	L
S	X	K	S	Z	B	H	K	W	U	Y	G	L	V	C	F	U	Q
T	R	Y	X	V	D	O	G	S	D	E	N	M	A	R	K	J	O
M	F	C	M	E	N	P	Y	U	G	C	M	X	S	T	C	F	B
P	V	A	U	S	T	R	A	L	I	A	O	H	P	E	L	C	R
Q	A	N	V	H	K	X	E	F	T	E	T	F	A	A	Y	W	A
I	C	H	I	N	A	T	J	F	W	M	F	M	I	I	M	J	Z
I	J	R	D	R	T	I	Z	I	W	E	B	U	N	H	P	K	I
Z	U	D	P	J	N	D	Z	G	H	N	H	N	B	S	P	R	L
U	H	A	I	T	I	X	Y	X	W	D	G	N	U	Y	F	S	K

COLOMBIA
NIGERIA
DENMARK
AUSTRALIA
SPAIN
HAITI
CHINA

HOST SPOT:

Also hidden is the country hosting the 2027 Women's World Cup. Do you see it?

....

Answers on page 74.

CHAPTER 7

DOUBLE DELIGHT

The 2024/25 campaign would finish with a double celebration for **Chloe**. However, the first half of the season was the opposite – one of the WORST times in her career!

Even though she was a top star for Manchester City and could win a game with a SPECIAL SHOT or a SLICK SKILL, **Chloe** struggled for regular action. From October onwards, she was only a substitute in City's WSL games and had ZERO goals in the league.

Chloe felt frustrated and hoped to leave City in the January 2025 transfer window.

Manchester United were keen to sign her, but City wouldn't do a deal with their rivals.

Then, on the very last day of the transfer window, a SENSATIONAL TRANSFER to Arsenal on loan was agreed.

The 27-year-old was back at Arsenal – the club she had first joined at the age of 12.

"YOUR ROOTS PULL YOU BACK."

That's what **Chloe** said about her amazing return to Arsenal.

She was so happy to be playing for a great team again, and alongside her England teammates **Leah Williamson**, **Alessia Russo** and **Beth Mead**.

++++++++++

Chloe's first game was a 5–0 THRASHING of Tottenham. It was 2,815 days after her last appearance for Arsenal back in 2017!

Her FIRST GOAL was in her next WSL game, which was a 4–3 VICTORY over West Ham.

++++++++++

Playing Champions League football was another big bonus at Arsenal.

Two assists from **Chloe** against Real Madrid in the quarter-finals helped put the team into the semis, where they then beat Lyon.

Could **Chloe** and her new teammates beat Barcelona in the final?

YES, they could! **Chloe** started the match, and **Stina Blackstenius** netted in a famous 1–0 win. Arsenal were the CLUB CHAMPIONS of Europe.

Now it was time for **Chloe** to defend England's title at UEFA Euro 2025!

+++++++++

At Euro 2025, held in Switzerland, 16 NATIONS

competed. England were the current champions, thanks to **Chloe's** winner in the Euro 2022 final. Regular football at Arsenal meant the Lionesses' coach **Sarina Wiegman** picked **Chloe** for the tournament.

The first group game against France was a poor result. **Chloe** played the last 30 minutes in a 2–1 loss.

England were rocked, but bounced back to DEFEAT the Netherlands 4–0. Their last group game was a 6–1 TRIUMPH over Wales.

Chloe had been a sub with no goals or assists . . . but that soon changed.

At 2–0 down against Sweden in the QUARTER-FINALS, she came on in the 77th minute to rescue England! Her cross was met by **Lucy Bronze** to score a header.

Then, in the 81st minute, another PERFECT CROSS by **Chloe** was knocked down for **Michelle Agyemang** to make it 2–2.

Chloe also scored a CRUCIAL PENALTY in the shoot-out before England eventually won.

Italy were England's semi-final opponents, and **Chloe** was again the GAME CHANGER in a cracking contest. After coming on in the 77th minute, she watched **Agyemang** score in the 96th minute to make it 1–1.

With just SECONDS left in extra time, **Chloe** stepped up to take a PENALTY. It was saved, but **Chloe** kept cool to score the REBOUND!

Thanks to her, England won 2–1 and had reached the final. The Lionesses were just ONE WIN away from being Euro champions once more.

Trying to stop them was Spain, AGAIN – a repeat of the 2023 World Cup final.

Chloe had been one of England's top players, but in the final she was on the substitutes' bench.

This time, with Spain 1–0 up, **Chloe** came on in the first half for the injured **Lauren James**.

Did **Chloe** have one more MATCH-WINNING performance to give? Definitely!

Another great cross by **Chloe** set up **Alessia Russo** to level the score at 1–1 . . .

. . . then after EXTRA TIME, and with the match still at 1–1, it went to PENALTIES.

The tension was off the charts!

In the shoot-out, there was a MEGA MIX of strikes scored, saved and missed, and even a re-take of England's first penalty. **Chloe** needed to score the team's fifth spot kick to win the trophy.

Pressure?
WHAT
PRESSURE?!

Chloe stood by the ball, did her special run-up, and blasted her kick into the roof of the net.

The Lionesses ROARED to victory!

The team went wild as England became EUROPEAN CHAMPIONS for the second time.

Chloe Kelly had delivered again in the biggest game of her life.

After the final and her brilliant penalty, **Chloe** said, "It's a huge moment. Every girl out there with that dream – you can do it. Keep shooting for the stars."

That's why **Chloe** is a . . .

FOOTBALL LEGEND!

SHOOT FINAL WHISTLE! QUIZ

Well, footy fans, that's it! How did you enjoy finding out all about the legend that is Chloe Kelly? Is your brain bursting with facts, stats and other cool info about one of the Lionesses' greatest players? Let's find out! Can you answer all 10 questions below . . . ?*

1. What European trophy did Chloe win with Arsenal in 2025?

2. How old was Chloe on her Arsenal senior debut?

3. What was the northwest club she played for on loan, before joining permanently?

4. What trophy did Chloe win for Manchester City in 2020?

5. At what stadium did Chloe score the winning goal in the Euro 2022 final?

6. Chloe netted the winning penalty in the Finalissima. Which country was it against?

7. In which year was Chloe a World Cup final runner-up?

8. How many WSL goals did Chloe score for Manchester City in 2024/25?

9. Before Chloe joined Arsenal's youth team, which other London club did she play for?

10. Which team did Chloe score the winner against in the Euro 2025 semi-final?

HOW DID YOU DO?

*** All the answers can be found in the pages of this book, and if you get stuck, the solutions are on page 75. But no peeking!**

0–2 correct: FOOTBALL BEGINNER.
Strong start, have another go!

3–4 correct: FOOTBALL ACE.
Nice work, baller!

5–6 correct: FOOTBALL WHIZZ.
Keep it up!

7–8 correct: FOOTBALL CHAMP.
There's not much you don't know about the game!

9–10 correct: FOOTBALL LEGEND.
Nothing gets past you. That's total **Chloe Kelly** quality!

QUIZ ANSWERS

End-of-Chapter Quizzes

Page 32: NAME GAME

1. NI**K**ITA PARRIS

2. BETH M**E**AD

3. MIL**L**IE BRIGHT

4. A**L**EX GREENWOOD

5. RACHEL DAL**Y**

The missing letters spell the surname KELLY.

Page 42: TRUE OR FALSE?

1. TRUE

2. FALSE (She beat Everton.)

3. FALSE (It was against BK Häcken.)

4. TRUE

5. FALSE (She was playing Birmingham.)

Page 52: GAME CHANGER

Page 62: TEAM TRACKER

```
. . . . . . . . . . . . . . . . . .
. . . . . C O L O M B I A . . . . .
. . . . N I G E R I A . . . . . . .
. . . . . . . . . . . . . . . . . .
. . . . . . . . . D E N M A R K . .
. . . . . . . . . . . . . S . . . B
. . A U S T R A L I A . . P . . . R
. . . . . . . . . . . . . A . . . A
. C H I N A . . . . . . . I . . . Z
. . . . . . . . . . . . . N . . . I
. . . . . . . . . . . . . . . . . L
. H A I T I . . . . . . . . . . . .
```

Host Spot: Brazil

SHOOT Final Whistle! Quiz

1. Champions League

2. 17

3. Everton

4. FA Cup

5. Wembley

6. Brazil

7. 2023

8. 0

9. Queens Park Rangers

10. Italy

CHLOE KELLY

PLAYER ACHIEVEMENTS

- England: Euro 2025 winner, Euro 2022 winner, World Cup 2023 runner-up, Finalissima 2023 winner, Arnold Clark Cup 2023 winner

- England Under-20: Under-20 World Cup 2018 third place

- Arsenal: Champions League 2024/25

- Manchester City: FA Cup 2019/20

THE VOICE OF FOOTBALL

SHOOT